CHERYL SWINTON WESTON

EXTRA, EXTRA,

WRITE

ALL ABOUT IT

You Don't Have To Be A Genius To
Write And Publish Your Book

Issues of Life Series

Published by: Cheryl S. Weston
Grace Us Living Publishing
Copyright © 2015 by Cheryl S. Weston

Library of Congress Control Number: 2015915937

ISBN 978 09832 18715

Printed in the United States of America

Anyone who loves the power of "WORD", would want to make a craft of it.

-Cheryl Swinton Weston

TABLE OF CONTENTS

With Heartfelt Thanks

I dedicate this book to the one who first saw my writing abilities, and was bold enough to challenge me. You planted the spiritual seed that germinated and provoked me to "write that paper." Your persistence and encouragement is the result of this book, and every publication resource that comes forth in the earth. Thank YOU!

Reverend Daniel L. Simmons

Because of your example of unconditional love, faith, and wisdom,
I have learned to go beyond and above mediocrity!
No amount of words will ever express the measure of my love and gratitude!

You are my hero!
God Bless Your Life!
Rest in Peace…

DEDICATION

To every person who has a story to share with the
world…

ACKNOWLEDGMENTS

To God and His Amazing Grace, thank you!

To Apostle Sammy C. Smith, thank you for your spiritual impartation.

To Tottie and The Ambitious Girl Movement, You ALL inspire me to keep building! Thank you for your tenacity and persistence!

To Karen Smalls Horlback, thank you for your demonstration of passionately pursuing your dream. You are truly a 21st century virtuous woman of many rivers! Your motivation and drive inspires me to keep building!

To J Senay Spurgeon & the Queendom Affirmation Movement, thank you for sharing your "DADDY's LOVE" with the world! Keep Building. You inspire me!

To every person that stepped out of the box and applied action of fulfilling your dream and vision, thank you!

To every challenge, trial, and tribulation, thank you for helping me to grow...

INTRODUCTION

Extra, Extra, Write All About IT was written to share good and bad news about writing and publishing your very own book. The purpose of the book is to encourage and provide both spiritual and practical steps to those who have dreamed about writing and publishing. The truth is, yes you can accomplish it! Many people have never gotten started because they disqualify themselves, and allow negative thoughts to stop or hinder them from making their writing dream become a reality. There are many misconceptions that can deter and stop you. One misconception is that a person have to be smart, intellectual and a genius. Well, that is not true! You don't have to have any special qualification. The only qualifiers is that you simply have to have a message, story or an idea that could be the solution to a problem, and be willing to share it with the world.

This book shares my personal testimonies about the everyday problems and issues we experience on a daily basis. The lessons learned after going through the process of each experience, can often help others find solutions to their problems. As I searched for answers to many of my own problems and issues, I eventually discovered the supernatural freedom and power of writing and publishing.

Ultimately, pain from trials and tribulations, led me through a spiritual metamorphosis Sometimes during my most difficult times, it was often hard to read scriptures and pray. I found solace in emptying out the pain and sorrow out of my heart and onto paper. As I journeyed through different spiritual seasons, I learned many of life's lessons and developed principles to live by. I discovered that on the other side of some of the problems and issues, I wanted to share the lessons learned. I became convinced that maybe at least one of my testimonies or stories could be a solution to someone else. Would you believe that maybe at least one situation, testimony or story, you have experienced, could help someone else in solving their problem? Everyone have at least one story, or have had a life experience that could help someone or be a solution to a problem? Their testimonies could be turned into life changing devotionals, stories, and self-help books.

Unfortunately, many people dismiss the thoughts for many reasons, and frankly. I did the same. It was after years of doubting, I took action of turning some of my testimonies into books. I can relate because it seemed so challenging. It took a lot of reflection, researching and commitment to compiling and writing spiritual growth and development resources. After years of spiritual torment and conviction, I became passionate. Boldness rose up in me that ignited me to make it happen.

Ultimately, one of my purpose in sharing my experiences and what I learned is to help others detour or prevent some of life's most gut wrenching pain and trauma. I realized that some of life's pain we must go through to gain the experience. Reflecting back to some of my most uncomfortable seasons, I can honestly admit that I went through some of them because of my disobedience and lack of spiritual knowledge and understanding. Some of the difficult experiences in life we have to be processed through, to gain spiritual understand; but we do not have to go through every one of them! The pain from some of the difficult times, I wouldn't wish it on anyone! Yet, it was those valley experiences that ignited my writing and publishing journey! There are many who share similar testimonies and stories, but are fearful in sharing through writing and publishing.

Extra, Extra, Write All About It was written to encourage and challenge those who have lived through situations that can be turned into spiritual growth and development books and self-help resources. This world is filled with people that have many problems. They are in search of solutions! You could be the change agent through your publications. No, you don't have to be smart or a genius to accomplish it. There is no special qualifications except loving God, people and this wonderful world He created. It took me a while too to realize that I did not have to be famous or smart to get it done. I simply had to surrender my heart and will to God, pray for guidance and write. Sharing the good and bad news of my experiences and the lessons learned was all that it took.

First of all, to get started, action is required! As you begin to identify the countless small and large lessons that life teaches, during good or bad times. Ask God to give you the boldness to put them in writing. Some lessons are learned consciously and others unconsciously, and during the most challenging seasons. Great life changing books can be developed. Get yourself a notebook, and begin journaling or writing where you are in your life. If you are in a very difficult season, write what you are feeling! There is absolutely no perfect time to begin! The lessons learned in your dark seasons, can help someone get through theirs. Life is an amazing school, and is filled with lessons that promote growth and development. Principles for life can be adopted and implemented to produce a better quality of life. When we take these lessons, write and publish them, others' lives are enriched, transformed and changed.

The process of writing and publishing can be daunting, but *Extra, Extra WRITE All About IT* shares good and bad news that will help you move from simply being a dreamer, and becoming an author. Yes, lives can be impacted by encouraging, teaching, and inspiring others through your book. The good news is this book gives you the support that will silence the dream killers, help build your confidence and gives the basic steps. You can make your dream of writing and publishing your books become a reality. It is time to stomp out all the misconceptions! Ask God to go with you on this journey, and pick up your pen and begin writing!

CHAPTER ONE

DREAM KILLERS

One of the first things you need to be aware of as an aspiring writer and author are dream killers. Dream killers are the number one cause that keeps a manuscript hidden and never becoming a book. There are many dream killers in the world. Basically, they are the negative thoughts we think and the negative influence of others opinion. Sadly, we allow what people say to penetrate our minds and paralyze our ability to carry out our dreams and visions.

Dream killers can prevent writers from becoming authors. There is a difference between writers and authors. Writers are dreamers who write out their dreams on paper, but authors are courageous enough to complete their work. Dream killers prey on writers that are immature, lack self-confidence, and can be easily distracted and defeated. Authors have more drive, persistence and tenacity. They are not afraid to place what they write in front of others to read. The difference between the two is simply their level of confidence and belief in their dream. Unfortunately, writers can be their own worst enemy, by killing their writing dreams, without even realizing it. Which one are you? Identify them, so you can get past being a writer and grow into becoming an author.

Dream killers do not always present themselves in the disguise of an enemy. Some are "well-meaning" people, like relatives and friends that are closest to you. Often, they are convinced that they know what's best for you. The truth be told, some dream killers are people who do not have a vision or dream; or simple fear following their own. Many possess the religious mindsets, and are those who cannot see any vision outside their culture, local church and community. The have lived inside their comfortable box and are afraid to step out of it. Anything outside that box is not reality because they themselves have never experienced anything else. They panic at the idea of coming out of their box, and they will warn you if you are trying to come out of your own box. Actually, they don't have a dream. Yet, we allow their opinion to sometimes stop us dead in our tracks and prevent us from completing what is dear to our hearts.

When I first announced that I was writing my devotional, a "well meaning" dream killer approached me. They warned me not to invest a lot of money in my book project because people may not buy it. Another handful of well-meaning dream killers tried to talk me out of it. They tried to

convince me how hard it is to make a living as a
writer and that the work would be unsteady. They
didn't stop there, but brought up that there are no
career benefits, and I'd no longer have health
insurance or a 401(k).I felt disappointed, but didn't
exposed my feelings of discouragement to them, but
I smiled and nodded. I told them I understood the
risks.

Dream killers will always be a part of your life.
They will offer you advice that you don't ask for or
need. It is always good to be polite by listening, but
sometimes you just have to find an excuse to get
away from them! In order to save your dream,
sometimes you have to run, literally! I would give
them feedback by telling them the rewards would be
much greater. Other times, I didn't respond.
Actually, each time I was approached by dream
killers, my heart grew more passionate to pursue my
dream of writing and publishing. I wanted to see my
dream come true. I continued on my path
determined to prove them wrong.

The truth is, every day naysayers talk people out
of pursuing their dreams. Taking charge of your
writing and publishing dream and becoming the
captain of your own ship isn't easy. Those that are
easily persuaded from pursuing their dream, may not
be well suited for the challenges that come with

writing. As hard as it is, we have to silence the negative voices that keep us from taking risks and pursuing our dreams of writing and publishing. Sadly, sometimes those voices are our own.

Do not underestimate the power of dream killers, they recognizes those with low self-confidence. It is much easier for dream killers to prey and plant doubt in the minds of new writers. Their ultimate goal is to keep your story and book from reaching the intended audience. Its objective is to convince you that you and what you have to share, is not good enough. Sadly, there are many gifted and talented writers out there thinking that they are not good when it comes to writing. Many people write books, but they never get it published. What's ironic is that the same people struggling and insecure with their dreams of writing, encourages and lead others toward their dreams and visions. In fact, the people they encourage to follow their dreams may not be as good at what they do. Yet, when it comes to their own abilities, they lack self-confidence to carry out their dream. These persons could be suffering from what is called a "Dunning-Kruger Effect. What that means is people who *are* actually good at something tend to *underrate* their abilities and may as a result, suffer from lack of confidence. Could this be you? I can relate to the theory.

Another enemy that could kill your dream of writing and publishing is trying to reach perfection too soon. By all means, perfection should be our main goal, but it comes with practice and time. You are not an expert until you have experience. Doing something repeatedly, produces perfection and excellence. Reaching perfection is the process of growth and development. There is no way that a child can operate and produce at the same level as an adult. They have to learn and grow. It is the same analogy in writing and publishing. Dreams dies when we expect the beginning, initial or early stage of a product to be perfect.

The beginning of anything is never perfect. In some cases, it is not even good. Practice makes perfect. I remember a saying that the old folks used to say, 'child, you have to creep before you walk'! I must confess! I know I am not the best at writing and publishing, yet! In fact, I am far from it, but the more I do it, the better I will become. I declare, Grace US Living Publications and Cheryl Swinton Weston, will be one of the best in writing and publishing! Begin declaring today!

A big mistake people make is giving up on their project, when they receive negative feedback after their work is completed. Their confidence in usually shot and they stop working on it. They put it down or bury it and give up on the project. For instance, the first publication I completed was about seven years ago. Looking back, I can honestly say that it was awful. I didn't think so because it was the first thing I had finished. I was proud of it, but not many others were. I didn't sell much. In fact, I gave most of them away because I wanted people to see it. I knew some people I gave it to talk negatively about it behind my back. I got very little positive feedback on it, but my goal was not to give up!

Well, I could have very well put it down and buried it. Instead, this year I revised the same devotional, put in on amazon, and sold more this time around. It is better, still not fantastic, but I can see the improvements. In fact, that same devotional has one thousand preorders from people I don't even know. Anyone that dream about writing and publishing, must learn to encourage themselves! I developed my very own motivator (motto) that keeps me focus to keep building. It keeps me encouraged and focused in realizing that everything and everyone is a work in progress. In fact, that is how God sees each and every one of His Creation. My motto is, *'Anyone who loves the Power of WORD", would want to make a craft of it.'* What that means is, because I love the powerful effect of the Word and my testimonies, I will continue to write and publish

IT until each resource gets better. The point is, never give up on any project or anything that is in your heart. Even if you don't get the rave reviews you expect, nor turn out the way you expected. My advice, put it aside, rethink the process, and I guarantee, you could make it better. God is not through with it yet. God does allow us to go through negative outcome, to build our self-confidence.

Never abort your dream by comparing your work with other writers and authors. Keep in mind that each of person is at a different experience and maturity level. When we compare our work against someone who has been in the game for a long time, you will devalue your *work* and think it does not measure up. We make comparison by allowing pre-conceived ideas and standards, evaluate the style that is in our heart. Your ideas should not be like everybody else! God may want to do something different through you. Sadly, we often model and compare ourselves with others.

The deadly dream killer is the copy cat! For instance, if I allowed where I came from, how I speak, and the many flaws I have, my dream of writing would never take place. I think we all have been guilty of comparing and measuring ourselves (according to societal views) with other more prominent speakers, preacher and writer. I am not what others would consider the best speaker, teacher or preacher. Some may have similar titles, but the delivery method may be different, but each person can accomplish whatever God created and assigned them to do. It's simply having the desire to learn, grow, develop and take action. Anyone or anything that continues to grow will get better. How we receive criticism too is a sign of growth. By no means confuse constructive criticism with dream killers. Constructive criticism are design to build you, not crush you!

When a person can recognize their flaws and work to improve, that is a person that is well on their way to perfection and excellence! For example, I am the first to admit, I have many flaws! I am very opinionated, not politically correct, and does not consider myself a great speaker, nor good at English. I had to walk down some rough roads because of those attributes. Persons with these type attribute, are not always received well. Many people have preconceive ideas, and therefore judge you based on assumptions. Never allow the negative views of others, cause your dream to die. Always invite God with you on your journeys, pray and let Him take the lead! To accomplish anything in life, you must trust God. He will continue to remind you of your purpose and value.

When I couldn't shake off my strong desire about writing and publishing resources, I knew God had to have had a plan, and was doing a new thing in the body of Christ and the world. I didn't grow up as a reader, but I have discovered that my desire for books began when I met Jesus! That may sound like a rehearse clique that we repeat because we have heard others say, and we say it because it sounds good! But it is true that my curiosity, and passion to know Him increased. When I went in search of His miraculous love and power, my lack of self-confidence diminished. My mission is simply sharing with others what I discovered about Jesus. The power of His Word eliminated my doubts, fears and insecurities, and fueled my passion and ability to write and publish.

Finally, another enemy that will kill your dream, is convincing yourself that you don't have enough to say to make up a book. A big misconception is what constitutes a "book." Let's define what a book is. A book is a collection of ideas, thoughts, experiences and facts with written and printed pages glued or banded together along one side and bound in covers. *(Cheryl Weston's definition)* Some people have believed that a book must contain a certain amount of pages; that is not true. If your ideas, thoughts, experience and facts is only twenty pages, that is your book.

Sadly, some authors won't consider writing a book that has less than one hundred pages. Actually, it would be a waste of time writing a three hundred page book and your audiences are non-readers. A question I ask my clients is, if the people that will purchase your book are basic or minimal readers, why would you write a three hundred page book? Your readers will have a greater possibility of reading and completing the book, the less number of pages. Ultimately, a book simply tells your story, view or idea, but it has nothing to do with the amount of pages or specific qualifications.

Apparently, God has put the dream of writing and publishing in your heart. It simply may be locked up because of various restrictions in your heart. When you make the physical move in the process of writing, it will help you move past your fears, insecurities, doubts and wrong beliefs. Unfortunately, dream killers will never completely vanish, but God has put the desire in your heart for you to accomplish for others, as well, as an eternal benefit. It's very clear in Ephesians 2:10. It says: "we are His workmanship, created in Christ for good works, which God prepared before we were even born to walk in them".

Ultimately, dream killers aim is to convince you to not write and publish your book. The world is filled of them, are close to you, and won't go away. You must recognize them and not allow them to kill your dream. If you are a person with a vision or a dream, they will always be a part of your life. The good news is that you have the power within you to disarm and dispel them!

GOOD NEWS

- ✓ There are many dream killers in the world. Basically they are the negative thoughts we think, and the negative influence of others opinions.
- ✓ Dream killers are the number one cause that keeps a manuscript hidden and never becoming a book.
- ✓ You must simply learn to disarm and dispel dream killers!

QUESTIONS

1. Can you identify any dream killers that have kept you from writing? Name two of them.

1. _____

2. _____

WRITE ALL ABOUT IT

_____
_____
_____
_____
_____
_____
_____
_____
_____
_____

ACTION PLAN

1._____

2._____

3._____

CHAPTER TWO

IT'S NOT TIME TO SHARE

Sharing your thoughts of writing and publishing too soon, could discourage and distract you in your early stages of completing your book. The act of writing has two phases, a private or solitary, where outside opinion or scrutiny seems like a threat. The second is a public or social phase, where the danger lies in being undermined or ignored. Personally, I am secretive by nature. I do not believe in letting others know what I am doing too soon. I have learned from past experiences that often when people who don't have your best interest, could work against you when given too much information. Ultimately, most writes prefer one or the two phases. My opinion is that you should never share your desire to write and publish too soon.

Basically, we should be knowledgeable of the different type people that make up our lives. The ones that are related by us through blood or by association. Some can be very negative and positive. The bible clearly states that we should know those who labor among us. When we have this awareness, be very selective on sharing your thoughts about writing to others. The least amount of people you tell about your dream of writing a book, the better.

Some may not agree, but I am totally convinced that it is best that some people don't know until the book is completed, and actually have a copy in your hand. I am not saying that you should be paranoid and not trust those around you. Neither am I saying that everyone is out to destroy your dream or vision. What I am saying is that many of the people that are part of your life have known none or fewer authors. They will doubt if it can be done because they may not have known anyone who could accomplish writing and publishing a book. Therefore, their unbelief has nothing to do with your ability, but it has to do with their lack of belief. Most of them will not believe you. Don't take it personally; but save your breath, passion and energy for accomplishing the completion of your book.

One of the very few people that could see my potential as a writer, was Reverend Daniel Simmons. He saw my ability to write before I did. Months after he became pastor of the church I attended, he recommended me as a delegate for the annual conference. After the church conference voted me as church delegate, my responsibility was to go to the conference and bring back a detailed report. Reverend Simmons challenged me and made it clear that he expected a well detailed report. He was a leader that was extremely serious about his ministerial duties and expected nothing but the best when representing God. He was serious about ministry, people's lives, and did not tolerate foolishness when it came to handling God's business. I had never remembered having an assignment like that put me under so much pressure, except while in high school. Well, the report turned out much better than I expected. In fact, the church gave the report rave reviews. After that, he kept encouraging me to write.

The first year after being ordained, at the annual conference, Bishop Preston Warren Williams II, challenged me to write a paper on evangelism. During the ministerial roll call, I was asked what part of ministry was dearest to my heart. My answer was street evangelism! I was given the task of writing about encounters and experience in the streets while evangelizing. Reverend Simmons kept pursuing me in getting it completed. After researching and writing, that paper turned into a book called, "Calling the Church to the Street". I must admit, I am little ashamed to talk about it because the book cover and manuscript have been completed over a year ago, yet remains on my computer ready to be in bookstores. Shame on me! In fact, every time I think about Reverend Simmons, I am disappointed in myself for not getting the book in bookstores. I felt worse because Reverend Simmons never lived to read it. He was one of the Emmanuel Nine in the Charleston church massacre. I must admit that fear and procrastination is the cause of that book still being on the computer.

I feel sometimes that a life of writing and publishing is like one of a preacher. It is often a lonely and a narrow place. The key is staying committed and faithful in carrying out the Great Commission of both assignments. The point to this story is, even without encouragement from others or a cheerleading team cheering you on, it is your responsibility to stay focus and get your book in print and in bookstores. Sadly, very few people will recognize your ability to write and publish a book until they see it. Frankly, seeking approval from others, shouldn't be your purpose for writing anyway. To save yourself from the least amount of disappointment as possible, write and publish the book, then share how it was accomplished! My view may sound harsh, but don't expect to get a lot of encouragement, if any at all. Don't take it personal if you share that you are writing a book, and the people you expect to respond positively, does not! It is simply not the best time to share your book journey.

On the other hand, promoting your book early in the process is best for your book's success. That's discussed more detailed in the last chapter. Promoting your book is different from sharing your ideas and thoughts about writing it, hoping that you will gain approval and support. People's reaction should be the least of your concern at this point in your book journey! Whatever people's response, don't spend much energy and time on that. Until they see the book, they won't believe! Ultimately, they may believe that a person have to be famous or a genius to write a book or become an author. Ultimately, stay focus to the completion of your project, and you will make a believer out of them when you complete the book. Take one day at a time.

One story in scriptures that help me understand the reasons for not sharing dreams too soon, or with those who lack vision. The story about when God chose Moses as His leader to free His people from bondage and out the hands of Pharaoh. Moses assignment was to lead God's people from Egypt and from bondage. The Israelites had always been oppressed and never experience freedom. They didn't know how freedom felt, nor looked like because they never experienced it. It is the same example for many today. Until people physically see or witness certain things with their own eyes, they simply won't believe. This is true also about the process of writing and publishing a book. God may have chosen you to write and publish a book for the same reason God chose Moses. When you accomplish writing and publishing your book, people will see; and that could set the people around you free! The world is filled with problems and issues and people are looking for solutions. What better instrument God uses, but you? You are someone that they can see, feel and touch. These are the one that probably have known you most of their lives, and could be set free and begin to go after their dream.

There are many people with gifts, talents and abilities, but are unaware of them. Some will die and go to their graves and never discover who and what they carry. Don't be one of those persons. You must begin writing and recording on paper what is in your head and heart. It could help someone discover who they really are. Just like God used Moses, he could be using you to set His people free. When others see your book or publication, they will also be free. They will no longer think that it may be impossible for them to release the gift God placed in them. You could be the first author they live to witness. Therefore, don't worry about sharing your dreams, just make it become a reality. Physical copies in your hand and on bookshelves, would make a believer out of them. Can I get a witness?

GOOD NEWS!

- ✓ To protect yourself from dream killers, be very selective on sharing your thoughts about writing to others.
- ✓ Most people will not believe you when you tell them about your dream of writing and publishing a book.
- ✓ Save your breath, passion and energy for accomplishing the completion of your book.

QUESTIONS

1. Is there anyone you believe you know if you share your dream about reading, could give you constructive advice? YES____NO_____

_____

WRITE ALL ABOUT IT

_____
_____

_____

_____

_____

_____

_____

_____

_____

_____

ACTION PLAN

1._____

2._____

3._____

CHAPTER THREE

YOU DON'T HAVE TO BE A GENIUS

Another good news is that NO, you do not have to be a genius to write and publish your book. The word "genius", according to Wikipedia, it is a person who displays exceptionally superior intellectual ability, creativity, or originality typically to a degree that is associated with the achievement of new advances in a domain of knowledge. Domain of knowledge is knowledge that is specific to an application, as distinguished from general strategic or control knowledge that is independent of the details of any particular application. Who I am and where I came from is evidence of that you don't have to be smart or a genius to write and publish. First of all, let me share with you a little bit of my background. My domain knowledge came from praying, researching and more researching on how to write, publish and promote my book. It certainly doesn't take a genius to go in search for answers and applying action to what you find out.

Personally, I didn't come from a family that is well educated or have lots of money. In fact, you didn't see a lot of books in my home. In fact, there were very few that were readers in my family. Two of my sisters, Helen and Trisha were readers, but it wasn't until my late thirties, I took an interest. I am the youngest of seven children, and my mother spent most of her time sometimes working sometimes up to three jobs in order to provide the bare necessities. I finished high school, but it wasn't until I was forty-five that I went back to college.

My goal was to get a bachelor degree by the age fifty, instead I earned a master's degree. By the time I finished college, the only person in my family that had ever earned a degree was my Aunt Juanita, as a registered nurse. My older brother, Joseph was the first to earn a bachelor degree. By the time I earned mine, I was the third in the family to earn secondary education, but the first to earn a master's degree. So you see, I didn't come out a family of educators or scholars, nor was I born with a silver spoon in my mouth. Knowing my background should convince you, that if I can write and publish books, anyone can.

Let me point out that in this book, I make reference several times to preachers, I do so because I am one. Therefore, keep in mind, I am writing from the perception of who I am, a minister of the Gospel. By no means, do I intend to exclude others or showing favoritism. Anyone and everyone have a testimony or life changing story to share with the world.

I do believe that God places a hunger for the Gospel in a person's heart, because He knows that you would go in search of an intimate relationship with Him. When I began my journey as a preacher, I became really hungry for studying His Word, books and becoming educated. Some preachers do not think that education is necessary to preach the gospel, but I tend to differ. Furthering my education was part of my spiritual, professional and ministerial journey. The more you know, the more you grow, and the better qualified to feed God's people. I didn't inquire about continuing my education until I believed God had a calling for excellence and leadership. He gave me the mission of equipping the saint for the work of the ministry. The goal and objective of the mission was to lead His people to spiritual maturity. Preaching and teaching His Word is my assignment.

One of the African Methodist Episcopal (AME) Church ministerial credential requirements is that candidates must have a Bachelor degree in order to become ordained as a minister of the Gospel. I had no problem with that. I wanted to represent God with my best. I felt I couldn't do that without learning all I could learn. I was called into the ministry about thirteen years ago, and have received two ordination. It wasn't until seven year ago, I realized I had the ability to write and publish books to enhance my ministry. My calling became clearer as a preacher, teacher and about my ministry, as I grew spiritually. Ultimately, the Holy Spirit is the Teacher and Guide. Yet, without the Spirit, that lives on the inside, the ability and passion to write and publish books, would be impossible.

God called and chose me to be a part of the church. Jesus Christ established the church to be His Body on the earth to bring to completion to the work He began, the work of reconciling the world to God (see 2 Cor. 5:18-19). When we accept Jesus as Lord, we are to proclaim His death, burial, and resurrection. We are to teach His Word, make disciples in His name, and exhibit His life. I understand that there are many ways to carry out this mission. Writing and publishing is just an added advantage to help teach God's people more proficiently. He not only gave us the command or commission us to proclaim and teach His Word, He also gave ministry gifts to us to enable us carry out our assignment. The five-fold ministry, Paul lists them in Ephesians. It was He (Jesus) who gave some to be apostles, some to be prophets, some to be evangelists, and some to be pastors and teachers, to prepare God's people for works of service; so the body of Christ may be built up until we all reach unity in the faith and in the knowledge of the Son of God. God's people must become mature, attaining the whole measure of the fullness of Christ. (Ephesians 4:11-13). We all are given different gifts, but they are to work together to equip the people of God. Therefore, my spiritual assignment allows me to write and publish spiritual growth and development resources that will equip the saints (spiritually) for the work of the ministry.

The term, "call to the ministry" simply means that He has called and gifted (equip) men/women to carry out the ministry gift for the building of the church. In my opinion, you don't have to wear a collar, wear a robe or carry a title. The qualifiers includes going through the sanctification process. It is when we go through that process that prepares one for leadership. I am sent to preach and teach in many different ways, not from a specific (physical) place. Our gifts enable and empower us to operate through the Holy Spirit. For example, for the past seven years, I preach and teach God's Word, predominately through my writing and publications. As I grow and develop spiritually, God is still perfecting my writing in this season by allowing me to operate in various roles as a preacher, life coach, writer, ghostwriter and publisher.

Ultimately, God has given me a mandate and mission of encouraging preachers, teachers, leaders, and those with a life changing story to enhance their ministry through writing and publishing. Some believe that I am hard on preachers, but it's only for the reason of provoking them to write and publish. God expects the church's leadership to be responsible for helping those they lead become more efficient in reading and spiritual growth and development. Ultimately, reading is door to the answer to people's problems and issues. I believe that when preachers write and publish resources, this could encourage people under their watch, to begin to read more.

Yet, every leader does not have the ability or time to write and publish. There is help in getting it done. If you are that person that need help, there are many publication services available. Your main part in the process, is becoming aware and taking the needed steps to begin the process of making your resources available.

My opinion is, people retain information better when involved in individual reading or small group learning. I can attest, when I attended school, I soaked up and absorb more knowledge. As a result, I gained more understanding when I participated in group studies or alone in the confinement of my home or in my own personal space. Likewise, people learn and understand scripture better in bible studies and smaller groups. In these type atmosphere, there are opportunities to discuss, share views and ask questions. I won't get into which method of learning is best, I simply want to point out that reading and understanding is key, no matter the method.

When leaders write and publish books, it helps the body of Christ to gain better spiritual growth, development and understanding. Making resources available promote spiritual development. Ultimately, the delivery of messages, sermons and bible studies are needed, but when we put lesson's learned in publications, it will change lives. No, you do not have to be a genius! In fact, anyone from any background, race, creed or color qualifies! The good news is that the only requirement is to get a pad and pencil, and begin writing or journaling your thoughts, ideas and feelings!

GOOD NEWS!

- ✓ The only requirement is to get a pad and pencil and begin writing or journaling your thoughts, ideas, and feelings!
- ✓ It certainly doesn't take a genius to go in search for answers and applying action to what you find out.

✓ Having ear to hear what the Spirit of God, having the passion to accomplish it, and allowing God to use you.

QUESTIONS

1. Is there something that's in your head or heart that may be your book or publication?

   _____

   _____

WRITE ALL ABOUT IT

_____

_____

_____

_____

_____

_____

_____

_____

ACTION PLAN

1. _____
2. _____
3. _____

CHAPTER FOUR

GET IT OUT OF YOUR HEAD AND HEART AND ON PAPER

Another great point is to begin writing down what's in your head and heart. The process of writing and publishing can be tedious and boring. You have to be committed and dedicated to what you are writing in order to make it to the finish line. Your biggest concern at this point should not be to try and figure out what's next, but capture the moments that you need for the meat of your story. Writing and/or recording your thoughts at the time you have them is crucial. Those thoughts are a part of your story. You can't see the flaws in what you are writing until much later on, but first you must start writing your ideas down.

The sooner you begin getting it out of head and heart, the quicker you will kill your fear of exposing what is being written. My biggest fear was that my book would be rejected and wouldn't live up to expectations. You must trust what you have in your head and heart enough to expose it by writing it. Stop putting off until tomorrow, tomorrow rarely comes. Don't allow fear to hold you back from getting that idea, thought or story out of your head and on paper. Put it down on paper and if it doesn't work, get another sheet and try again. Sooner or later you will be convinced that you do have something valuable to share in a book or publication.

First, you have to avoid the little demon called fear. Dismiss him by going to the store and buying a black and white composition book. That's my favorite type, but any notebook would suffice. Once you have it home, find a good pen or pencil and a place, inside or outside, where it is quiet. Put your pen to paper and begin writing whatever comes to mind. Pick up your pen and gets those thoughts out of your head and hearts and record them on a paper! Don't just lift the pen, but keep it on the paper. What you write doesn't have to relate or make sense. Just keep writing.

The main purpose is to get a free flow to whatever comes to mind. Eventually, your mind will become settle on what you want your book to be about. Just keep writing. The longer and more you move your pen, the rhythm and movement of the pen, will seem to unlock your mind. Yes, I may sound too elementary about it, but actually getting a notebook and picking up the pen and writing is the most difficult task to begin writing.

In the beginning of your writing journey, many things will not make sense. It will appear like you have bits and pieces of sentences and paragraphs of mumbo jumbos and incomplete sentences. Keep in mind, during this process, you are only collecting thoughts and ideas. Later on in your writing and publishing, it all will begin to make sense. Don't get lost in this process. Many people get lost because they try to make sense of it. They think that nothing could possibly come out of what they are writing. If you keep writing, you will later discover and identify your purpose in writing and publishing.

Getting your book out of your head and heart and onto paper means whatever you are experiencing and thinking. The thought are important and they are not just idle thoughts. Write them down. You may not understand at the time all of your thoughts, but as you begin to pray and submit to the leading of the Holy Spirit, you will understand later on. Do not try to understand or make sense out of everything. Remember that the purpose of the Holy Spirit is to lead and guide you into all truth. Therefore, the first thing you must recognize is that your negative thoughts is your biggest enemy, and will try to stop you from completing your book. The power of our thoughts can either help or hinder us. It all depends on what you are thinking. Our thoughts are often connected to our well- being and the direction of our life. It is indeed a battle to get your thoughts out of your heart and head and onto paper.

The world is full of many people who are afraid, would give up and not pursue their dreams of writing. They sat back with frowns and skeptical stares with no determination whatsoever. Writing a book sounds far-fetched to many. Their favorite words are "Why should I try? Nobody I know ever has"? They have already memorized the rules and their minds are closed to new and creative desires and goals. Their focus is limited to 'I can't, I don't and I won't'. Scriptures reminds, "As a man thinketh so is he (KJV). Keep in mind that your mind is the enemy's target because the mind holds the secret of soaring.

We are what we think and will accomplish what's in our thoughts. If you are having doubts about getting your ideas out of your heart and head and putting it in a book, go ahead and put some action to your thoughts. Resist the feeling of doubt and insecurity. The Greater One (Holy Spirit) lives on the inside of you. He puts no limit on you. You limit yourself. Get a pad and pen and begin to write down anything you think of. What I do to help me get pass negative thoughts is go on the computer or laptop, and begin setting up and outlining the new book. Try it, it may motivate you to start writing or go to your next process in writing and publishing your book.

Don't worry about who will or won't read it or if it sounds right or not. At this point in the game, you have no one but yourself to be accountable to. There is no audience to entertain and no customers to keep happy. Lastly, beware that there will be times that you feel stuck and don't know what to write. This is called "writers block". Don't panic. This happens to all writers and authors. When it happens to me, I pray and ask the Holy Spirit to lead me and keep me on track. Writers block will pass and you will begin to write again.

Another way to get it out of your head and heart and onto paper is by saying it out loud and recording it. Yes, you can write by recording. Get a recorder. There is probably on your phone. One of my favorite way of getting it out of my head and heart and onto paper is by speaking what I am thinking, and later go back and write is down. My most precious and best thoughts come early in the morning. It is important not to miss the moment. If I don't capture my early morning inspirational thoughts and ideas, I will lose them. Therefore, I pull out my phone and begin to speak.

Recording is also a great idea because sometimes the thoughts and ideas come so quickly. It is nearly impossible to write fast enough to capture them all, therefore, speaking helps to capture all. When time permits, or later on when you have more time on your hands, you can transcribe the audio into digital form. People who are extremely busy, hire someone to transcribe or a transcriptionist, but at this point, don't worry about that yet. Just keep on capturing your thoughts. Personally, I transcribe my audio myself. Periodically, you may have to remind yourself that you are on an adventurous, but learning, journey. Don't turn your journey into hard labor. There is not a right or wrong way. Have fun and enjoy your journey. When you get to the ending stage of compiling your book, more ideas comes. This allows you to use the material to become an intricate part of your book or any publication resource.

Don't let the little demon of fear defeat you. Recognize and defeat him in the beginning. Get your materials ready, start writing and complete your book. You must take action (pick up pen/pencil) and face your biggest fears. The good news is that what you hold in your head and heart could be the solution to someone's problems! FEAR won't stand a chance!

GOOD NEWS!

✓ You have to be committed and dedicated to what you are writing in order to make it to the finish line.

✓ It is indeed a battle to get your thoughts out of your heart and head and onto paper.

✓ Don't let the little demon of fear defeat you. Recognize and defeat him in the beginning.

QUESTIONS

1. Is there something that have been on your mind that could be a part of your story?

_____

_____

WRITE ALL ABOUT IT

_____

_____

_____

_____

_____

_____

_____

_____

ACTION PLAN

1._____

2._____

3._____

CHAPTER FIVE

GOD GAVE THE WORD, GREAT IS THE COMPANY THAT PUBLISH IT...

Ultimately, every believer of Christ is called to spread the Good News of Jesus Christ. There are many ways to communicate God's Word, and that include writing and publishing. It is simply spreading God's Word. All scripture is given by inspiration of God, and is profitable for doctrine, for reproof, for correction, for instruction in righteousness (2 Timothy 3:16). The function of the WORD, according to this verse, is to equip believers with ALL the wisdom and morals they will ever need in living a successful life for Him. If your life is successful, righteous, perfect and fruitful for Him then your life is worth living. To accomplish this, He has given us His Word, His Mind, which is the Mind of God Almighty. The Word causes us to think His thoughts, and to judge with His judgment. Every believer's mission is to publish the Word of God, and this can be done through, preaching, teaching, and writing.

The scripture became clear to me when the Holy Spirit deposited Psalms 68:11 in my spirit. I had never heard the scripture. For the past couple of years the Holy Spirit had been tugging at my heart about planting a writing and publishing ministry. I was hearing, but continued to find excuses of why I couldn't do that. God always remind us of what we should be doing. The Holy Spirit is awesome, but if I was to be honest with myself, sometimes I try to avoid Him. I must admit that my disobedience happens whenever I feel unqualified to do a job God assigns me to. Amen church! Can I get a witness?

If I would describe the Holy Spirit, my description would be that of gnats or fruit flies. God buzzes constantly in your ears, up your nose and is persistent when He wants to get our attention. Like bugs, when we try to ignore Him, He won't let us. It is very difficult to brush off when He gives us a task. He will not leave you alone until you get in the correct posture and position to accomplish it.

I could not wait to go home and look up Psalms 68:11, when it was released to me. "God gave the Word, great was the company that publish it." As I sat in church that Sunday morning, I began to take my usually notes of the message for the morning. Every assignment from God is uncomfortable, but I knew I was in my spiritual place. I always felt a strong stirring and really energized, when I was operating in my lane of gifting. The battling with the doubts and fear was constant about whether I truly could write, and publish or was this just an illusion of mine? I had been taking notes now of Apostle Smith's teachings for at least a year. I had enough notes to write several books. Negative thoughts taunted me and tried to convince me that I wasn't qualified to do it. Everything that came out of the Apostles' mouth, by the time I got home and reviewed what I had, the Holy Spirit would give me ideas on how to publish it.

I could remember my first year; Apostle Smith announced of the upcoming consecration month. He called it "The 31 day Ezra Fast", and immediately, I thought of putting it in a thirty-one day fasting devotional guide. The logic was, if the body of believers could have this guide, it would help them understand more about prayer, fasting and consecration. I had been in church long enough and witness scriptural and doctrinal lack of understanding. That included myself. I was born and raised in the church, yet many things I didn't understand. Providing this spiritual growth and developmental resource would bring a clearer understanding to the purpose of prayer, fasting, communion, etc. I had learned that teaching why we celebrated certain observance, activities and programs in the church, is so necessary and important. Many churches have programs, but the body do not have a clue reasons why. When it comes to fasting and prayer, more need to be taught. Fasting would produce more power in our life and the corporate church. My heart desire was in connecting my gift to the church in perfecting the growth and development of the church. Unfortunately, those closer to the Apostle, took offense and fought hard to kill the publication ministry.

I was new to the ministry. It seemed the first sight of me, the people that basically ran the church was already treating me as an enemy. No, it wasn't my imagination! I kept writing, avoiding and having the least amount of physical interaction as possible. I guess the ones that seemed to oppose my presence the most, could be called one of the clicks of the church. Their eyes were always on me, looking to prove their mind provoked, and baseless allegations. In my opinion, church clicks overall mission was keeping people out of church that needed to be in church. The more I ignored them, the more aggravated they became. The longer I stayed, the more attacks and harder they came against me. In spite of all their efforts to abolish me, I knew I was there on an assignment. I wasn't going to allow them to run me off until my mission was completed!

The time I spent in my personal prayer time sustained me. I was a regular attendant of the church's corporate prayer meeting. What was ironic, most of the people that attended, were a part of the church click. They were the ones Satan was using to try to get rid of my presence. What do you do when the click actually made up the church's prayer meeting? Better yet, they were the church prayer ministry! WOW! In fact, one of my group spiritual attacks took place at one of the prayer meetings. The attacks didn't work. I had been through too much hell in my lifetime, to let the enemy bluff and scare me in running from this assignment! Undoubtedly, many times, I just wanted to take my pen and paper and like Apostle Smith would say, 'Get the ham and cheese', up and out of there. I wasn't going to let the spirit of the clicks prevent me from my assignment. I had to stay focus and committed to get all I was hearing and putting it on paper. God gave me His Word to publish!

When on assignment, you must keep moving forward and building. Doubt and fear is a constant enemy. The enemy didn't want me to believe that I was smart or anointed enough to accomplish it. God was building the writing and publication ministry with His Word. He had already deposited the name in my heart. Gracious Living, but spelled "Grace Us

Living". Psalm 68:11 was the foundational scripture of Grace Us Living Publication. God strategically kept building my confidence, affirmations and confirmations. I knew I had to totally depend on the Holy Spirit to lead and guide me in my next move.

The next thing I did was research the scriptural meaning. The "Word" literally means the bearer of (good) tidings. In some translation it is used as a feminine form and translate it as women, For instance, in the ESV it says "the women who announce the news", while others discard the gender, (KJV) says "the company of those that published it". According to Clarke's Commentary on Psalms 68:11, it says, "Great was the company of those that published it of the female preachers there was a great host." Such is the literal translation of this passage; the reader may make of it what he pleases. Some think it refers to the women who, with music, songs, and dances, celebrated the victories of the Israelites over their enemies. But the publication of good news, or of any joyful event, belonged to the women. It was they who announced it to the people at large; and to this universal custom, which prevails to the present day, the psalmist alludes.

Understanding this scripture helped me to make sense and convinced me of what my ministry consist of. I began to understand the personal and agonizing pain, trial and tribulations, I had to endure. The "whys" I had asked God, for many years, became clearer. It was until I went through the process of healing, I realized I was going through a process of getting clearer understanding of the meaning of Psalm 68:11.

As I struggled with my daily issues and problems, I would search out scriptures that would encourage and get me through some of the horrible times in my life. I finally realized it was the Word of God that delivered, healed and restored me in every situation. During some of my most horrific seasons, it was difficult for me to pray sometimes. There were times when I couldn't utter a word. I discovered journaling my thoughts, feelings, emotion, writing down prayers was the medicine that soothe the pain and agony that was in my heart and soul. Writing was my way of releasing the pain and expressing my feelings.

I discovered everything I had experienced, contained messages, lessons and principles to live by. My purpose was to write about them to help others. I had to go through the process and get healed before sharing the experience with others. Eventually, after the process, I understood my purpose in life was to preach and teach, but also write spiritual growth and development resources to help and teach others, the Word of God. These publications should solve problems, bring healing and produce spiritual maturity. The same holds true for many of you. Recognition is the first step toward your writing and publication ministry.

When I first recognized my ability to write, I didn't quite get how it would fit in with my call to preach. I was raised thinking that being called to preach included preaching from a pulpit on Sundays, reading scriptures, praying, visiting the sick, administering communion, performing funerals and weddings. Actually, my impression came from what I saw preachers around me do. As time went by, I grew and develop in understanding what my calling was really all about. I can remember when I preach my initial sermon. I will never forget that day. I felt so in tune to the Holy Spirit and on fire for God. My sermon text came from Luke 9:23, *"And he said to them all, if any man will come after me, let him deny himself and take up his cross daily and follow Me"* (KJV). Reflecting back to the day I preached it, I had not a clue what I was talking about. Today, I would teach and preach it totally different. The main points and lessons I would convey would be completely different. Time, space and experiences, have launched my view of the scriptures.

A part of my spiritual growth and development came from the research and studying scriptures. In preparation for preaching a message or teaching a workshop, by the time I had my sermon or message outline, I would have enough life changing information to write a book, devotional or a self-help spiritual growth and development resource. I wanted to share what I found out with those who were experiencing the same or similar situations in life. I believe that was one reason the Spirit made me aware of Psalm 68:11. I was the company (person, ministry) that publish (share, tell, write) how God's Word delivered and healed me through the things I encountered. People would be able to relate to what I was writing. I was a tangible (see, visible, now, today) source they could relate to.

God began preparing me for the writing and publishing ministry (Grace Us Living Publications) while growing up in my home church, Olive Branch A.M.E. Church. My passion for teaching others began with teaching Sunday school. I went from teaching catechism to young adult in a couple of years. God's favor allowed me to start the church group childcare program, assisted the sunbeam choir, began a community small group women's prayer group (The Power of a Praying Woman), and wrote an adolescent and teenage girls program called "Young Women of Virtue". It mentored and taught adolescences, teenage and young adult females the importance of inner beauty, holiness and purity. My preparation journey continued with opening my own daycare center, and wrote the curriculum of that program. I used my gift in keeping the Sunday school bulletin boards up to date, wrote vacation bible study curriculum, member of the Education Achievement Award Committee and made the booklets, chairperson of the Mother's Day Committee for six years, Praise and Worship Leader, New Member Class Leader and teacher, Evangelism Leader, wrote and published curriculum and training manuals for almost every ministry I became involved with.

I realize that God was preparing me for what I now understand as one of my calling. In this scripture, there were all examples of God providing His Word, but His expectation was to spread what His Word says by communicating and publishing IT. God inspired us to make these resources available for others to read over and over again.

As God inspired men to write His Word, we are His people that are responsible to publish it? Not only did God give His Word, but His Word has great power. God's Word is more important than anything else. It sustains us no matter what we go through in life. His Word is sent to heal us from all of our infirmities. Matthew 24:35 reads, "Heaven and earth shall pass away, but my Word shall not pass away." Psalms 138:2 says, "...for thou hast magnified thy WORD above all thy name."

The origin of God's Word (Bible) is a collection of books which were written from ancient times to Roman times by various men in various places. The bible is compiled by history, poetry, prophesies and instruction. It all fits and works together because the Spirit of God is the One and Only author. I believe that everything God allows to happen in our lives, He intend for His Glory to be revealed. His Word is the guide for our lives. It will carry us through the difficult, as well as the good times, but we are to write testimonies about how the Word has deliver us.

Grace Us Living Publications was established for that same reason. It came out of the passion for writing and publishing. Our mission is to help leaders and those with a story to write and publish it. It is a well-known fact that writing and publishing added to preaching and teaching can help people grow and develop into spiritual maturity. We have been called to equip the saints of God and give them the tools they need to become the change agents of this world. Every born again believer are the change agents of the world, and our good, bad and ugly experiences have equipped and qualified us to solve problems and issues. In fact, after studying church growth and history, some of the most influential leaders were all authors. God sees those who know Him as being great to communicate and witness of His goodness and mercy.

GOOD NEWS

- ✓ Every believer of Christ is called to spread the Good News of Jesus Christ.

- ✓ There are many ways to communicate God's Word, and that include writing and publishing. It is simply spreading God's Word. It is indeed a battle to get your thoughts out of your heart and head and onto paper.

- ✓ It is the Word of God that delivers, heal and restores in every situation. Don't let the little demon of fear stop you!

QUESTIONS

2. What does Psalms 68:11 means to you?

_____

_____

WRITE ALL ABOUT IT

_____
_____
_____
_____
_____
_____
_____
_____
_____

ACTION PLAN

1._____

2._____

3._____

CHAPTER SIX

MAKING THE BEST SELLERS LIST *SHOULD NOT* BE YOUR MAIN FOCUS

Making the best sellers list is an honor most authors would love to achieve. In fact, making the best sellers list is a measuring stick that keeps many great books from being published. It is a great achievement and promoting tool, but it should not be the main focus. Your main focus should be providing the best story or information for the audience your book will target. Books are written for many different reasons, but the ultimate reason should be, a solution to someone's problem.

Many people take years to write and publish their book. One reason could be that their heart motives is not for the purpose of their intended audience. Some authors want to accomplish for self-gratification, and impressing others. In this day and time, authors are becoming more visible, but in the past, a person was considered smart or a genius only if they wrote a book. They are many authors and books out on the market now, therefore, competitiveness changes some authors' reason for writing and publishing books.

No matter the reason, we should be exceptional in everything we do. Writing shouldn't be glorifying oneself only. One's purpose for writing and publishing should be for a bigger cause. The world is filled with people who are going through many problems and are simply looking for answers. Your main focus should be the people that could be helped through reading your book. When we think seriously about why and whose life our books will touch, making the best sellers list becomes less important.

It is true that sometimes books take years to unfold. The ending of a story often take time, and a writer can't bring it to an end simply because they want to. Becoming too anxious can be one problem why many books do not make it to publication. First time authors often try to run before they can walk, and these books never make it to publication. Their motive for writing sometimes is for selfish gains or to win a medal of honor. Their aim is to make the best sellers list. Ultimately, if a writer's reason for writing is not for the purpose God intended, but simply to glorify oneself, the book usually never becomes reality nor does it delivers what it is purposed to.

Writing and publishing is another resource leaders make available to enhance the growth and development of the people they lead. It is another vehicle a communicator uses to help those they lead, grow and develop. The reality is, God chooses and send leaders to those He has assigned them to. He knows what they need to make their life whole and healthy. He allows leaders sometimes to go through uncomfortable situations to gain experience and a message. God expect leaders to bring solutions to everyday problems through messages, sermons and publications. Whether the message is preached audibly or written, it should be communicated in a way that will reach and help those God intended them to reach.

God is always speaking to us. Anytime an individual attends a church, spiritual and business conferences or a workshop, the message that is taught or facilitated is usually for the people hearing and attending. I have heard messages preached and taught that was so life changing, I would make a comment like: "Boy, she should have been here to hear this message". Actually, the message was not for the people not in attendance. That is how strategic and all-knowing God is. He knows what each and every one of His children needs, but if our focus is not on the message, we will miss what the message is saying.

On the other hand, when leaders write and publish their message or sermon, persons not in attendance can purchase the resource to read later. The same process is true when we write a book. This is another example of the importance of why our main focus should not be on making the best sellers list. If our focus is off, your book would be another book without a life changing message. Of course, it is always great to make the best sellers list, but it's more important that it reach and help those who God has assigned it to reach!

A leader that teaches and preaches, the people you lead should be able to identify your teaching and preaching. Their perception of you, your beliefs and opinions is concluded from what you say or write. You are their leader and shepherd. The bible reminds us that," My sheep hear My voice, and I know them, and they follow Me. (John 10:27. The people you lead are like sheep. Sheep needs a shepherd. A shepherd rescues, feed, and lead. Your job or assignment is to lead by exhorting, edifying and building them up. He has chosen and sent you to provide His people with what they need to draw out, empower and equip them to function sufficiently, effectively and purposefully. As their leader, you should always be open minded to new and better ways of enhancing your methods of accomplishing the needs of those God has called you to lead.

The good news is that when you take your focus off getting on the best sellers list, your responsibility of leading your sheep becomes easier. The characteristic of a sheep is evidence of why God have appointed you as leader and shepherd. Many sheep wander around lost, sometimes within a few miles of its home. They have no sense of direction for finding the fold. A lost sheep will walk around in a state of confusion, unrest and panic. It needs a shepherd to bring it home. Likewise, it is the same for a person that is assigned to your leadership. When you write and publish growth and development resources, they purchase it, read and study your book. They no longer wander around lost. They gain deeper understanding in the areas they are undeveloped in. Understanding trumps out ignorance.

The more we understand God's Word and what's happening around us, the freer and mature we become. Therefore, as their leader, you have done your assignment because you have made available another vehicle to teach, preach, reach, rescue and lead them. Writing and publishing is simply another way to feed the flock.

We have heard many times that people like sheep spend most of their lives eating and drinking, but often don't know what is good and healthy about their diet. They are unaware of what is poisonous and non-poisonous. Therefore, the shepherd must guard their diet and provide them with nutrients that are rich. Spiritual food and healthy life principles are the healthy nutrients needed. Writing and publishing your books and resources will ensure your flock is being fed a healthy spiritual diet. Just as a sheep could get lost and go astray, that is also true for the shepherd or the leader, when they are not being fed properly.

When we focus on who and what God has sent us to, we won't get off our mission. When we stick to the plan, lives are enhanced, enriched and changed. Ultimately, that pleases God. Self-inventory should be habitual in a leader's life making sure that the Holy Spirit is guiding you and not the best sellers list. Trust the Spirit, He knows who will need to read your publications. The ultimate goal of your book should encourage, build, edify, exhort and be the solution from whatever problems and needs. A leader is responsible for taking who they lead to another level or to introduce them to a better quality of life. Your book or publication should shed and provide light to the dark area of their life.

More importantly, imagine how appreciative those you lead will be if they can go into any bookstore online, church or local bookstore to purchase the spiritual growth and development resources written by their very own shepherd or leader. Resources that extend beyond the sermon, message or workshop can add to their resource library. How excited they will be when they can purchase teaching and preaching from the vessel God uses to feed them His Word. The added resources will stimulate the body of Christ and they will stimulate one another through assembling in church. The good news is to give people hope through encouragement of the scriptures, and watch evangelism explode! Your books and publishing will extend your ministry, career or business. Can you see why your focus should not be on making the best sellers list? God has given you the charge and warns that those who fail to feed the flock are not fit to be shepherds (Jeremiah 23:1-4).

Lastly, when you commit your works (focus) unto the LORD, your thoughts will be established. (Prov. 16:3) You will take your eyes off the best sellers list. The power from this Word will help you to submit your focus to God. He will help you to organize your thoughts and strategies, and will reveal to you a solid plan for completion. The final result will benefit both you and your readers, you will realize that as you write, you are also learning. The more you learn, the better leader you will become. Ultimately, you too will be establishing more spiritual and physical authority!

Freedom lies in realizing that your first, second or third book may not be perfect, but it is important to keep your focus on the main points or message you want to convey. One of the enemies of completing a book is thinking that everything you write has to be perfect. A leader is not perfect, therefore nothing he writes will be. Yes, you are striving for perfection, and it will come close as you grow in writing. Do not allow your imperfections to keep you from starting, building and improving the craft of writing.

The knowledge and becoming skilled in spiritual warfare is vital. Like any other thing we battle for, recognizing that we do not wrestle against flesh and blood, but becoming skilled in combating and fighting spiritual thoughts that continually tries to rob us of our focus, is necessary. Silence all the chatter in your mind that tries to get your attention by speaking out the Word of God. Man's biggest problem is that whatever we lack, robs us of our focus. When we don't have the thing we need or it is not visible, it distracts and takes our focus because we want to see it with our physical sight. Not knowing how the final product of the book will be, causes us to doubt.

This negative perception comes from the thought that unless it is perfect or good enough for the best sellers list, it can't help someone. That is simply not true! Man expects perfection, but the Holy Spirit does not! Don't be afraid to write what the Spirit is revealing, even when it sounds contrary to popular beliefs or doesn't make sense!

The Holy Spirit will lead you into the direction He wants you to go. Sometimes, that could be an unchartered territory where no one has ever been before. That could be the area where the solution is found. Everything does not have to make sense or it may not look like or sounds like anyone else's. Always combat your feelings of discouragement and comparison. You will from time to time get discouraged. But the power of the Spirit that is on the inside of you, does not allow you to remain in that state.

For instance, I must confess that I have many books that are still on my computer. They are there, not because they are not finished and ready for publication, but I felt they were not perfect. There is a difference between a story that haven't ended and one that has ended. Never use perfection as an indicator as to whether a book is complete. Most writer and publisher may have a different opinion. Every person reason for writing is different.. Always let your compass or guide be the Holy Spirit. I do respect the rules of writing and publishing, but I strongly believe we grow only through the mistakes we make. On the contrary, many writers and publishers feel like every error must be gone before publication.

It is indeed very good if there are no errors, but some books would never get published if you let that be your main qualifier. It is okay if you find an error or if everything isn't perfect. Actually, every project or book you write will become better. You can't be afraid to put the book out there into the world. The saying, "Do not despise small beginnings" is true. The enemy sometimes uses the obsession for perfection to keep us from making available the book or resource that people need.

Sometimes if leaders are not careful, they exercise oversight of the flock by the example of his life. Those you lead should know that you are not perfect as a person or as a leader. Unfortunately, that could be why some pastors don't share in writing resources many of the gut wrenching testimonies that they have. Many leaders paint the wrong picture of who they are to those they lead. They give the impression that they don't struggle with problems and issues, nor make mistakes. One reason people are devastated and traumatized when a preacher's or leader's struggles and issues are exposed, is because they forget that they are flesh, and therefore are not perfect men or women. Many people think that leaders are free from struggles and problems. I do believe that sometimes, God allows a weakness to be exposed to see how those they lead will react or handle their leader after they have been exposed. A leader is never exempt from struggles, problems and issues. In fact, most leaders, especially preachers and teachers of the Gospel struggle more!

It is true that leaders must have standards and should have good character and integrity, but it is more important that a leader is chastened. They should be spiritually strong enough, but not hide their vulnerability and act as though they have none. Mistakes and errors are part of life and are actually tools that make us grow.

It is impossible to lead effectively without mingling and integrating with those we lead. You cannot be a leader that led from above, but to lead from within. An effective pastor or leader does not herd his sheep from the rear, but lead them from the front. They see him and imitate his actions. That is true in reference to writing. As long as your books have spiritual weight, your sheep will care less about a misspelt word or a simple error in your book or publications. In fact, making mistakes and errors will reveal to them that you are not perfect.

In an earlier chapter, it is discussed the importance of not sharing your dream early in your process of writing and publishing your book. People's negative views will kill your dream! Go back and read chapters (Dream Killers & It's Not Time To Share) as often as you need to. When you feel doubt and fear during your moments of feeling insecure, the best one to talk to is God. Naturally as humans, we need a human to vent to.

On the other hand, God usually have a least one person's shoulder to cry on when we experience overwhelming doubt and fear. Usually, God will send someone to help build your confidence so you don't give up. It is a lonely road for people with vision, drive and tenacity! I am not trying to scare you, but there are not many people that can see what you see. There are not many that have big dreams and expectations for their life. When you have a dream, it has to be protected because there are dream killers always lurking, waiting to kill yours. Look out for them. Be aware of them. Here is a hint and a brief description of one. Two things they will say if you reveal that you are writing a book, "You really think you can do that? Nobody I know ever did that before." The second thing they do. They may not respond verbally, but they get quiet! When pursuing any dream, sometimes you will feel like you are in a foreign land, all by yourself. So often, during times of loneliness, we forget that God is always with us. He never leaves us nor does He forsake us. During those lonely times, He is actually teaching, doing a work or perhaps even giving you another story that could actually be the best seller!

GOOD NEWS

- ✓ Your main focus should be providing the best story or information for the audience your book is targeted for.

- ✓ Those you lead will be appreciative if they can go into any bookstore online, church or local bookstore to purchase the spiritual growth and development resources written by their very own shepherd or leader.

- ✓ When our focus is off, everything about our life is put on hold.

QUESTIONS

1. Have you done an evaluation of your heart and reasons why you want to write a book?

    _____

    _____

WRITE ALL ABOUT IT

_____
_____
_____
_____
_____
_____
_____
_____
_____

ACTION PLAN

1._____

2._____

3._____

CHAPTER SEVEN

WHAT SHOULD I WRITE?

What you should write depends strongly on what's in your heart. What are you passionate about or is there a problem or an issue that really irritate you? Have you gone through a life experience and the lessons learned could be the answer to someone's problem? What is your purpose in life is or what your earthly assignment is? Ask yourself these questions honestly and the answers will tell you what you should write. On the other hand, if you don't already know, pray and ask God to reveal that to you. A good indicator could be simply asking yourself the question, "What would I do as a career, ministry or business, even if I didn't get paid to do? Your answer should be what you should write.

Searching your heart is another indicator to help you find out what you should write about. It is usually the thing you love to do so much, and you would do it even without being paid. Of course, you would eventually get paid as you discover, grow and build your brand. Knowing what you should write would help you in deciding. What are some of life's lessons you have learned? What are some of the things you know how to do and have become an expert in? Do you have a solution to a problem that could help someone else? Do you have a story to share or it simply could be a title?" Whatever you chose to write and publish, ultimately, you should have a passion to share or say something that could help someone through a difficult time.

For years, I went through many of the uncomfortable and unpredictable times and seasons. Suffering seemed to become a way of life for me. The biggest misconception was in believing that when I became a believer of Christ, my life would be wonderful. I wasn't told that all hell would broke loose. When problems, trials and tribulations began to take place, I thought I was being punish by God. I felt I wasn't doing something right. It wasn't until I found comfort in writing that my solution came. I spent many days and nights talking, begging and crying to God to get through some of the most horrific times in my life.

I discovered that writing down my pain brought me healing. Actually, my pain pushed me to writing! At times, the pain would get so horrible, it was painful to pray! I took solace in writing down the agony I felt. I discovered that journaling and writing became my Balm in Gilead. I found such great relief when I wrote down my feelings and prayers. Periodically, I would go back and read some of my testimonies. It ministered and helped me while reading. It finally occurred to me, what I was writing could also help others.

The first thing I wrote was the first women's devotional journal in 2008, *"To Know Him"*. I had just been through a few seasons of trauma, heartache and pain. I was a different person at the end of those seasons. I had grew and develop and my spiritual understanding increased. Grateful to God, I survived through them. I felt a need to share and help other women who were going through similar situations. I had not a clue about writing and publishing.

I was determine to do it and my passion was strong. Supernaturally, I could see myself holding it in my hand and giving it to other women to encourage them. After all, the main reason I was so adamant to write about it, was for those that were going through pain and sorrow. They had to know that the ultimate reason we go those difficult times, was for the purpose of knowing God. I named the devotional journal "To Know Him." All throughout my journey of writing it, I would get discouraged and wanted to quit. The more I fought against negative thoughts, the more I got closer to completing the project. It was by no means perfect, but I was so proud of it.

My goal was to write, publish, promote and print the entire book, including binding it. My passion was to complete the entire process from start to finish. I had very little money to buy publishing equipment, but I began purchasing one item at a time. My journal binding was spiral, so the first thing I bought was a paper cutter, a spiral binding machine and coils. I was preparing myself for the journal completion. The closer I got to finishing, the more excited I became.

When the time came for editing, I did that myself. Months earlier, I sent it to two of my friends to edit, but they never returned it. That was an indicator that they didn't read it. Honestly, I didn't know at the time that it wasn't good at all, but I began to rewrite and edit it again. I was convinced that my dream of becoming an author and publisher was no mistake, and that this was what God wanted me to begin with. I changed, rewrite, edit over and over again. Finally I was convinced that it was time to publish it. The content was good, but it did not seem to have much spiritual weight, but it was perfect for those who were still young in their spiritual walk. Actually, they were the ones who were really in search of getting to know God. I was fulfilled just knowing that God was still proud of my accomplishments. During the entire process, I didn't get much encouragement and accolades from people I shared my news with, but I knew deep within that

God was taking it somewhere. In fact, when I told people I had written a devotional, some looked at me like I had lost my mind. I sometimes felt discouraged, but kept refocusing to the goal at hand. I knew that once I finished the entire project, I was then qualified to say I was a writer and publisher. God would use my efforts of completing as a seed to the birthing of my publication ministry, Grace Us Living Publication!

My main focus had to be to complete the journal. Sharing through writing and publishing a resource for women who were struggling through their difficult season was my mission. It is crucial that you keep your mind off of things that did not matter, and staying focus to why and who you are writing it for.

Finally, I finished the project. I didn't sell many copies, but I wasn't concern about the money or time I had invested in this project. I had to complete this for God. It was as if I and He had an agreement. Even though the natural results didn't look impressive and it was far from making the best-sellers list, I knew it was bigger than me. My greatest desire was that the devotional would help someone get through their difficult time. It wasn't until I finished, I began to notice that even the people around me who knew of my journal didn't support it. They acted as if it didn't exist. The thought often made me feel bad, but whenever I felt down, I would check my heart motives for doing it. It was important to me that I wasn't doing it for self-glorification, but this indeed was an assignment was of God. It is easy to start with the best of intentions and end up wanting praises from others. I didn't want to write and publish for all the wrong reasons. As you begin to write, always ask yourself, "Am I really doing this to serve others or to serve myself?" The good news is, what you write about should be a heart matter! I hope by now, you have a pretty good idea what you should write about. If you have not, keep reading!

GOOD NEWS!

✓ What you should write depends strongly on what's in your heart.

✓ A good indicator could be simply asking yourself the question, "What would I do as a career, ministry or business, even if I didn't get paid to do.

✓ The good news is, what you should write about is a heart matter!

QUESTIONS

1. What are some of life's lessons you have
    learned? Can you name at least two?
    1._____
    2._____

WRITE ALL ABOUT IT

_____
_____
_____
_____
_____
_____
_____
_____
_____

ACTION PLAN

1._____
2._____
3._____

CHAPTER EIGHT

WRITING YOUR BOOK

If you are still struggling with what to write, the good news is that you can continue praying and asking God for guidance. It is a good idea to always pray before anything. I am the type of person that rely totally on God's direction. Personally, I am one of His children that humans may call nagging and sickening. I ask Him for everything, no matter how small it seems. Ultimately, whatever you write should help solve or give a solution to a problem. Basically, stories, self-help books and journals all aid in helping change people's lives. People are bombarded with many problems today, and are looking for quick fix and solutions. They are in search of resources and publications that they can easily pick up, and find answers to whatever they are faced with. Publication resources help people to grow and develop, and solve problems. When problems are solved, it brings healing and restoration.

Thinking about the book title is a great place to start. If a title don't come during this step, creating an outline is a smart way to guide and keep your book on target. You begin by writing down five to ten questions you would want your book to answer about the title. If you do not have a title yet, don't panic, it will come. Each of these questions will become your book chapters. This will be your book outline and it will serve as a guide to help you cover what you want your book to be about. This process will help organize your research journal notes and serve as a guideline when setting your personal deadlines for completion. Traditionally, most books have ten chapters, but it does not have to. You can add more or subtract, as least or many as you'd like. The number of chapters depends on how much or little you would like to say or cover in your title. If you follow those steps, at this point, you should have a book title and a list of questions which will become the chapters of your book.

Keep in mind that you should be journaling or writing down your thoughts in a separate notebook. These notes are the meat of your book and will play a very important part of personalizing your book. It is also extremely important to sit down and write a writer's plan. Habakkuk 2:2 reminds us that we are to, write the vision and make it plain upon tables, that he may run that read it (NKJV). The vision and outcome of your book would be very difficult to steer without writing a plan. Whether it is writing or publishing a book, all ideas, vision and project should involve planning. Planning is important if you want to be successful. It is a guide that helps identify goals, gives directions, uncovers problems, adds professionalism and gives perspective. When we plan, it helps us to stay focused, keep our perspective and carry out our goals of writing the book.

There are three categories of goals; short, midterm, and long term. An easy way to balance them is by getting a blank sheet of paper, write each column and categorize them. Short-term goals are those items you would like to see done in the next 2-3 days. These goals are quick, simple and easy to accomplish. The mid-term goals are things you'd like to accomplish in the next few weeks or months. This is the broadest time frame and is a little more difficult to estimate. Ultimately each should be well-defined so that it can be easy to carry out. Finally, the long-term goal is much more abstract and is the long term aspirations for your book or publication. Writing these goals out and organizing them into these three categories will give you the great beginnings to a roadmap of completing your book journey.

If you do not write a plan to navigate and keep you accountable to writing, you will not accomplish your goal of completing your book. Specifically, decide which day you want to write and stay committed to write at least one chapter a day. A good idea is to get a calendar and come up with a daily, weekly and monthly schedule.

Keep in mind, your ten topics is your chapters. Write one chapter a day. Write your plan on your calendar, the days and how much time you will invest on each chapter. Set goals and a deadline for each stage that lead to completing of your book. After you write the topic questions and the answers, next step is to expound on each answer. Interject examples, testimonies, stories, resources and information to validate your views. Don't worry about editing or rewriting anything that will come later. It is extremely important that you relay the message. Stay on topic. There's nothing worse than reading a book that starts with a bang, then runs off into a bunch of nonsense. Stay focused on your message from the first page to the last.

Planning helps you to do that and it offers you great direction to arriving at your next point. The more prepared you are, the better you are able to handle problems that arises. Proper planning also helps to uncover potential problems before they even occur. Your book journey will be more enjoyable if you can uncover possible bumps in the road. It is better to discover problems early on.

Planning will also help your book to be more professional. Professional doesn't mean stiff and dry, but fun and enjoyable. Professionalism is the result of being prepared. Preparation is another word for planning. Planning always adds a sense of professionalism to your book. Your book will always turn out better when you plan your course of action, outline your goals and when you uncover problems. Always give yourself the opportunity to be prepared for things that arise. Proper planning does not mean everything always works as you intend. There will always be errors, problems and failures that occur. On the other hand, planning helps you maintain your professionalism as you handle what is not expected.

Planning your books goals and direction helps to give you a clear perspective of what matters and what is possible to accomplish. Planning how to accomplish your goals will force you to organize them and also to prioritize them. No one wants to waste time working on something that is not important. However, the day to day life of a writer or author easily gets overwhelmed and those goals and objectives get lost in the daily grind. Do not believe in the fictitious stories of instant fame. Don't be fooled. The good news is that you will write a great book when you have an action plan, identify goals and move confidently towards writing and publishing your book. Maybe you will be the next author everyone is talking about.

GOOD NEWS!

- ✓ Whatever, you decide to write about it, put some action to it.

- ✓ The vision and outcome of your book would be very difficult to steer without writing a plan.

- ✓ Stay focused on your message from the first page to the last.

QUESTIONS

1. Do you know what you should write about? Can you list at least one idea? YES___ NO__

_____

_____

WRITE ALL ABOUT IT

_____
_____
_____
_____
_____
_____
_____
_____
_____

ACTION PLAN

1._____
2._____
3._____

CHAPTER NINE

STRUCTURING YOUR BOOK

You are now ready to structure your book. The good news is that structuring your book is taking what you have written and putting order or a form to it. You may be wondering: how do I transform this mass of content into something resembling a book? At this point, you should have the guts of writing and completing your book. If you don't, these are simple steps in accomplishing this.

First, make sure you have change the chapter questions to statements. These will become your chapter headings. The second step is taking an inventory of the content, everything you have gathered. Go through each chapter and do not be afraid to take some content out and save for another book. People who have been writing for years may have so much content they could write more than one book. Next, review your research. While structuring your book, you may realize that you are missing information and need to fill in places. Then, evaluate experience, testimonies and knowledge. Next make sure your story is well sandwiched. That means injecting your personal testimonies in each chapter. Doing this reconnects the reader back to you keep their focus.

The power actually is in a book that connects you to your readers. Make sure you explain the principles or lessons learned from each chapter. Evaluate any supporting stories that may be included in each chapter. Supporting stories are a collaboration or witness what you are saying or confirm any point that need to be made. In most cases, these are usually other people's story. Giving the readers real life examples keeps them interested. Most people learn and relate best by examples. Finally, evaluate the ending and summary of the book. Do this by recapping what the readers learned, include questions that will provoke and challenge the readers. Finish it by giving an action plan or a to-do plan.

Writers tend to think that structure is something that just happens, but it's not. Each chapter should have at least one main point. That doesn't just happen. It often takes weeks and months to decide on that structure. Once you have a structure, own it and work within it. Make it yours and stick with it.

As you structure your book, keep in mind that the start or beginning must be strong. The first chapter has to be really inviting. It must draw the reader's attention. Your first pages must be really good. When people pick your book up in a bookstore or see it on amazon.com or online, they look at the cover, at the subtitle and they check out the first page or two. If you haven't hooked them in the first few pages, they're not going to buy.

It is okay to revise while structuring, if you realize that something is off and that it's not going to work for you. Whatever structure you chose, stick with it. Be certain that you stay within the border of structure. A good structure acts as a roadmap through your book. It helps you to channel and shape your ideas and prevents them from running away with you. It takes a lot of the fear factor out of writing and will see you through to the end. When you follow a structure you'll boost your chances of producing successful books.

Finally, add an introduction at the beginning of your book. When I wrote my devotional journal, I wrote the introduction first. What I found out was, I had to revise it many times before I finished the book. An introduction explains why you wrote the book and how the reader will benefit from reading it.

Editing of course is a part of this process and you'll have to develop your own strategy. The good news is that if you find difficulty in structuring your book, a publisher, like Grace US Living Publications (GULP) can help you.

GOOD NEWS!

✓ Structuring your book is taking what you have written and putting order or a form to it.

✓ As you structure your book, keep in mind that the start or beginning must be strong.

✓ If you find difficulty in structuring your book, a publisher, like Grace Us Living Publications (GULP) can help you.

QUESTIONS

1. Have you reviewed all of your steps to the final writing process? YES_____ NO_____

   _____

   _____

WRITE ALL ABOUT IT

_____
_____
_____

_____

_____

_____

_____

_____

_____

_____

ACTION PLAN

1._____

2._____

3._____

CHAPTER TEN

HOW DO I PUBLISH?

Most likely, after structuring and editing, you've finished your book manuscript. Unfortunately, the final process is not completed. Many think they are finished, but until it is published, it still won't be in book form. At this point, you need to decide who will publish it or perhaps you want to publish it yourself. Whatever your goals are, you can research and find the information needed to get it published. The publication process consists of compartments and most companies provide services to complete the entire process. Actually, if you do not want to do any publishing, all you have to do is hand your manuscript over and they will give you a proposal on their services and prices. Make sure you do your research and are confident, if you decide to hire a publisher. Do your homework and search for the one that is right for you.

On the other hand, it is always good to know how to publish a book. Whether you are after the traditional publishing experience, complete it with an agent, editor, and publisher or want to self-publish your book, it's completely within your grasp. You decide what works best for you. Whatever you decide, I will guide you through the basic book publishing process, and give you the basic resources to choose which publishing option fits your need.. First, you should know about traditional and self-publishing.

Traditional book publishing is when a publisher offers the author a contract, prints, publishes and sells your book through booksellers and retailers. The publisher buys the right to publish your book and pays you royalties from the sales. If you want to publish a book traditionally, you will need an agent. Depending on the type of agent needed, you must identify the right category for your book or writing. You would submit a book proposal from three sample chapters for non-fiction. For fiction books, a manuscript must be submitted. After completing these steps, you must write a query letter to send to potential agents. For a more in-depth study of traditional publishing, do your research. Those are the basic steps in traditional publishing.

Self-publishing are writers who self-publish. In fact, in this age we live in, they are having greater success like never before. E-Book publishing, internet marketing and social networking sites have helped self-published authors get their books in front of readers and potential book buyers. When you self-publish, the control and success of your book is in your hands. There are many self-publishing options out there. It is up to you to research to find out your best option. While in traditional publishing, the publisher handles the marketing, distribution and warehousing for your book. There is no expense to the author and mainstream publishers make a profit from book sales. On the other hand, in self-publishing, depending on which type of publisher or platform you choose, the majority of the work falls on your shoulders and you pay for all expenses. The main advantage of self-publishing is that you control when the book is published, you retain all rights to your book, and you receive 100 percent of the profits. In both traditional and self-publishing, you have the option to choose what format your book will be published in, printed book, e-books, audio books, CD's, DVD's, and many more.

It is possible to be both, writer and publisher. This book is proof that you can do it. Grace Us Living Publications is a different type of publisher. Our mission and goal is to encourage and assist potential writers. Our services includes the publishing process. Currently we print through amazon, and all of our authors own their books and receive their 100% royalties after amazon printing prices. We simply coach, guide and transform your manuscript to book form. Our heart is spiritual growth and development resources and self-help resources. Whatever you chose for your publishing, do your research and chose what is best for you and your readers.

GOOD NEWS

- ✓ After structuring and editing, you've finished your book manuscript, but the final process is not completed.

- ✓ At this point, you need to decide who will publish it or perhaps you want to publish it yourself.
- ✓
- ✓ Make sure you do your research and are confident, if you decide to hire a publisher.

QUESTIONS

1. Have you decided what method of publishing is best for you? YES_____NO_____

_____

_____

WRITE ALL ABOUT IT

_____
_____
_____
_____
_____
_____
_____
_____
_____
_____

ACTION PLAN

1._____

2._____

3._____

CHAPTER ELEVEN

BOOK PROMOTING

Now that you have written and publish your book, there are many ways to promote it. The goal is to reach your audience. There are many ways to promote, but remember you only need to do one thing at a time. When you are consistent, it won't be long before you will be reaching your audience.

What I learned after publishing my first book was that it was better to start promoting before the book was finished. The most powerful and essential steps you can take toward promoting your book, begins long before the actual launching of the book. The best time is actually a couple of years before the book is published. The earlier you begin in building a network of supporters and reviewers, the better. It is always good to keep track of everyone you meet as you research and write your book.

Early in the process of researching and writing your book, a good idea may be, to start a blog. Add 100-150 words each day of helpful and inspirational information on issues in your field. Make sure they are related to the subjects in your book. Always pay special attention to and take notes about those who show enthusiasm for you and your project. A website is good for promoting also. Post sample chapters from your book, a link to the Amazon page for your book, so people can buy the book online, your media kit, book reviews, schedule of appearances, including bookstores, speaking engagements, conferences and contact information. The closer your book launching date arrives, keep in touch with these people. It is smart to send them an occasional email and keep in touch via a social networking site like LinkedIn, Twitter or Facebook. The most old fashion and simpler way to practice selling your books is one on one. Instead of trying to sell your book to faceless thousands, find one person who needs and wants your book. Offer your book to that person and keep on repeating.

Other ways of promoting your book could be by having parties and event for significant milestones, like signing your book contract, the completion of the manuscript and the arrival of the finished books. Those types of events could draw key people together for a house party. The author is his best promoter when it comes to selling your book. When you develop a positive attitude about book promotion, people will pick up on it, and tune in. Some writers resent the chore of promoting their book. Be careful not to exhibit an attitude, you are a writer or author, you shouldn't be promoting. Some authors have that attitude, especially if they have a publisher. They feel that promoting their book is the publisher's job only. Unfortunately, if you don't promote your book, no one else will.

Another idea of promoting your book is creating a media kit. Your media kit should include: professionally printed business cards with the book cover on one side and your contact information on the other side. It is a good idea not to print them on your home printer. Investing in your product and yourself, could pay off in the long run. Also getting a head shot by a professional photographer and a well written 100-150 biography that qualifies you to the book and reader. It is always good to include a few short recommendations from colleagues and friends in the description.

Lastly, create a pitch for your book or something like an elevator speech. Three pitches are ideal, 10 seconds, 30 seconds and 60 seconds. When someone asks what the book is about, give them the 10 second pitch. If the person responds and show interest, have a longer pitch ready! Practice your pitches on friends until they tell you the pitches work. These are just a few of the many ways you can promote your book. If this is your first book, keep in mind that you are now an author. Many new opportunities are waiting. New doors are open. Use the internet and other sources to find new resources.

Research, research and research where the opportunities are and don't be afraid of treading new territories. Remember, Stop procrastinating! *Extra, Extra, Write All About It!*

. **GOOD NEWS!**

- ✓ There are many ways to promote it. The goal is to reach your audience.

- ✓ The earlier you begin in building a network of supporters and reviewers, the better.

- ✓ Be careful not to exhibit an attitude, you are a writer or author, you shouldn't be promoting.

QUESTIONS

1. What are two ways that you can promote your book?

   1. _____

   2. _____

WRITE ALL ABOUT IT

_____
_____
_____
_____
_____
_____
_____
_____
_____

ACTION PLAN

1._____
2._____
3._____

Conclusion

I hope and pray that *Extra, Extra, Write All About It* have convinced you that you don't need anyone's permission to write a book. When you ask God to guide you on your writing journey, you will accomplish your vision and see your dream come true. Know that every human experience is valid, and the many lessons learned can be a solution to a problem. You must be convinced that what you have to say is most important. Let prayer be your guide, stay focus and get to work. Remember, every thought, trial, problem, issue is of some value.

Keep several notebook available, and everything that you write will connect eventually! Write what you are passionate about. Keep in mind that the stories that are the best, usually comes from some of life's most painful experiences. Be aware of the many dream killers that will try to stop you from writing and publishing. Dream killers' goal is to cause doubt and fear. His intent is that your book do not reach its intended audience. There are many negative emotions and distractions that will try to take your focus and prevent you from completing your mission.

It is the lessons learned from the uncomfortable, unpredictable and most challenging times, that makes the best stories. The ultimate goal of writing and publishing is in helping others find solutions to their problems and issues. It is a good idea to allow God to heal the wounds of hurt and pain that often are hidden in our soul. This would allow you to get past the shame, negative opinions and connotations that comes with pain and trauma. Then, you are free to write with confidence. You're the author, take charge!

Ultimately, it doesn't matter how much encouragement or books you read, the only thing that will ignite you to write is believing in yourself. You must be confident that you have something important to say. You must develop the confidence to believe in yourself. *Extra, Extra Write all about IT* is about my own personal journey. Following some of the suggestions and examples may help you to get you started on your journey.

This book is to encourage you and help you to recognize that you may have a story and you do not have to be smart or a genius to put it in print. It shares the pitfalls of writing and publishing that will try to prevent you from accomplishing your dream. These basic steps is only a guide. Ultimately, as you commit to writing and publishing, you will develop your very own style and method. Your mission is to write for your target audience, and to get your publications in stores, the internet and into the world. Remember, do not focus on making the best sellers list, only on those you are writing to. Just in case you do make the best sellers list, don't forget to mention this great resource. Someone is waiting for your book. It could be the answer to their problem. Don't make them wait too long. Get started! God bless you on your writing and publishing journey. Extra, Extra, WRITE All About IT!

ACTION PLAN

CHECK LIST

✓ _____

✓ _____

✓ _____

✓ _____

✓ _____

✓ _____

✓ _____

✓ _____

✓ _____

✓ _____

✓ _____

✓ _____

NOTES

The English Standard Version Bible. New York: Oxford University Press, 2009.

The New Oxford Annotated Bible. Ed. Michael D. Coogan. New York: Oxford University Press, 2007.

Peterson, Eugene H. The Message: The Bible in Contemporary Language. Colorado Springs: Nav. Press, 2002.

Zondervan NIV Study Bible. Fully Rev. Ed. Kenneth L. Barker, Gen. Ed. Grand Rapids: Zondervan, 2002.

Wikipedia

Adam Clarke Bible Commentary

ABOUT THE AUTHOR

Cheryl Swinton Weston shares good and bad news about her writing and publishing journey. She shouts loud and clear *"Extra, Extra, WRITE All About IT"* and hope it brings awareness to the many communicators, teachers, preachers, and leaders, to write and publish! She feels it is important for those with a testimony or life changing story, to unleash their writing power and ability to communicate in writing and publishing.

She has earned a Master's of Science Degree in Human Service and an Associate Degree in Early Childhood Education. She received her Itinerant Deacon Ordination in the AME Church and Elder Ordination in Grace Cathedral Fellowship. She is a Motivational Speaker, Certified Life Coach, founder and CEO of Grace Us Living Publications (GULP).

Cheryl loves to encourage, motivate and inspire others. She believes that every person have at least one story to share with the world, and that story could be the solution to someone's problem!

LET'S KEEP IN TOUCH!

For more information about the ministry of Cheryl Swinton-Weston and a list of available books, small group studies, publications, preaching and speaking engagement, workshops and CD messages, you may contact through email, twitter, Instagram and Facebook.

Grace Us Living Publications (GULP)
Email:graceusliving@yahoo.com
Website: www.graceusliving.com